Sunny Paradise!

LINEWORK PATTERN WORKBOOK

by Annie Lang

It's time to grab your beach gear, help yourself to a fruity beverage and head on over to enjoy a day in sunny paradise! You'll find dozens of mix and match tropical beach, surf and sand themed designs you can use to create everything from party invitations, summer vacation wearables and scrapbook elements to patio decorations and summer tableware.

Simply trace the design and then transfer the image onto your project surface to make outstanding personalized items with professional results every time.

Transferring the linework designs

Trace the design of your choice with pencil and tracing paper. Place transfer paper under the tracing paper and place onto your selected surface. Hold in place with tape if necessary. Retrace over the linework to transfer the design onto the project. For fabrics, trace the design, flip the pattern over and retrace the lines using a fabric transfer pen. Follow manufacturer's direction to iron the design onto your chosen fabric item.

Color or paint these designs with

Craft paints, watercolors, markers, coloring pencils, chalks, inks, fabric pens, paint pens, or crayons

These designs are great for

Home Dec Items like furniture, cabinets, accent items, walls, lamps, glassware, kitchen accessories, office and desk items, bathroom accents, cabinets, patio pots and outdoor items, etc.
Fabric and wearable items like t-shirts, sweatshirts, aprons, canvas shoes, totes, quilting squares, table linens and napkins, window and shower curtains, pillows, etc.
Paper Craft Projects like greeting cards, scrap page elements, tags, labels, stationery items, ornaments, gift bags, etc.

For more ideas and designer tips, please visit my Blog at
http://annielang-anniethingspossible.blogspot.com/
My Pinterest Board at http://www.pinterest.com/anniethings/
or my Facebook Page at
http://www.facebook.com/anniethingspossible

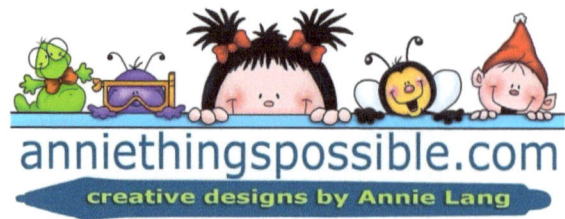

Annie Lang's
Fun in the Sun
Copyright (C) Annie Lang

Annie Lang's
Fun in the Sun

Annie Lang's

Fun in the Sun

Copyright (C) Annie Lang

Annie Lang's

Fun in the Sun

Copyright (C) Annie Lang

Annie Lang's
Fun in the Sun
Copyright (C) Annie Lang

Annie Lang's

Fun in the Sun

Copyright (C) Annie Lang

Annie Lang's
Fun in the Sun

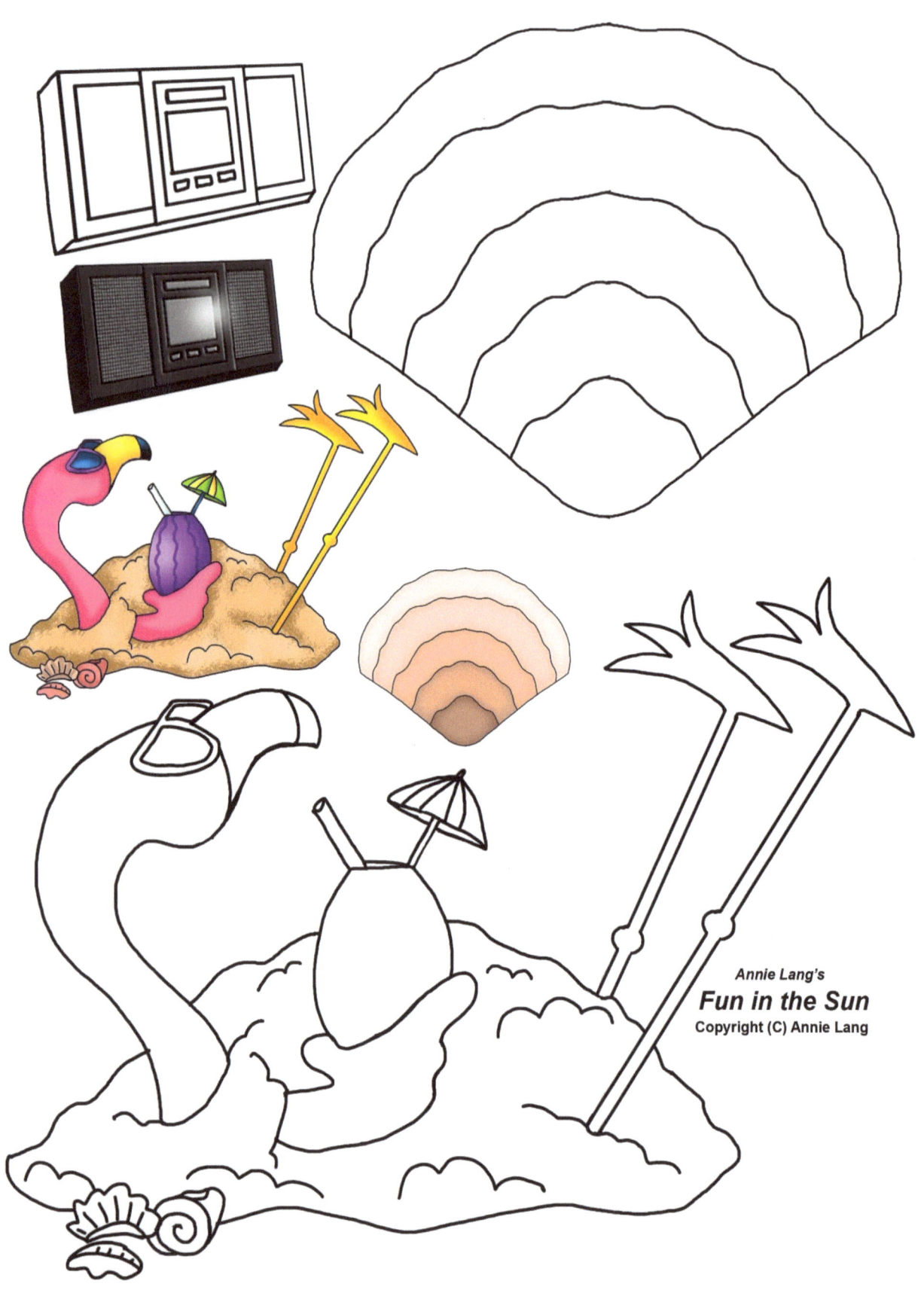

Annie Lang's
Fun in the Sun
Copyright (C) Annie Lang

Annie Lang's

Fun in the Sun
Copyright (C) Annie Lang

Annie Lang's
Fun in the Sun

Copyright (C) Annie Lang

(C) Annie Lang anniethingspossible.com

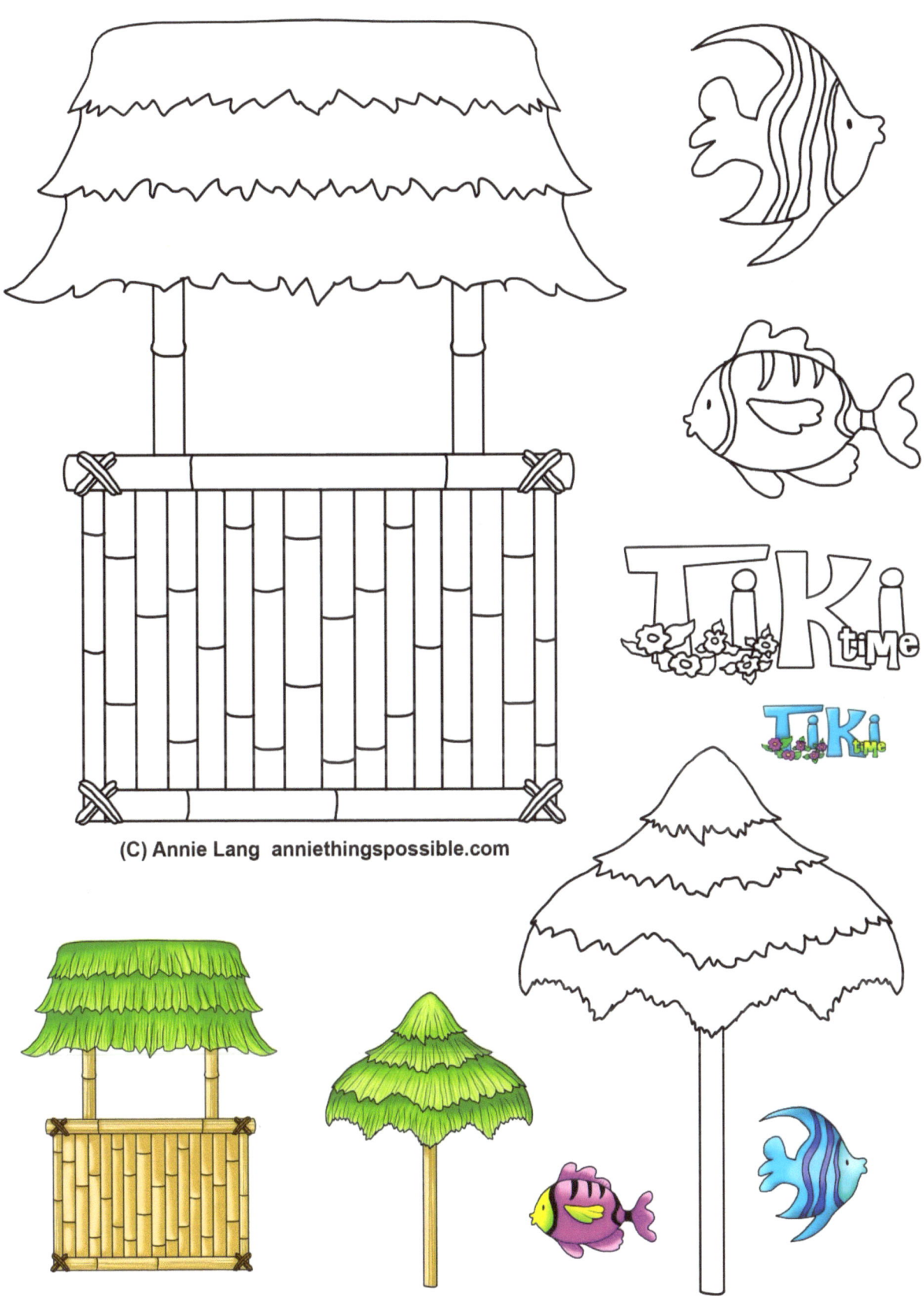

(C) Annie Lang anniethingspossible.com

PINEAPPLE PASSION

PINEAPPLE PASSION

PINEAPPLE PASSION

PINEAPPLE PASSION

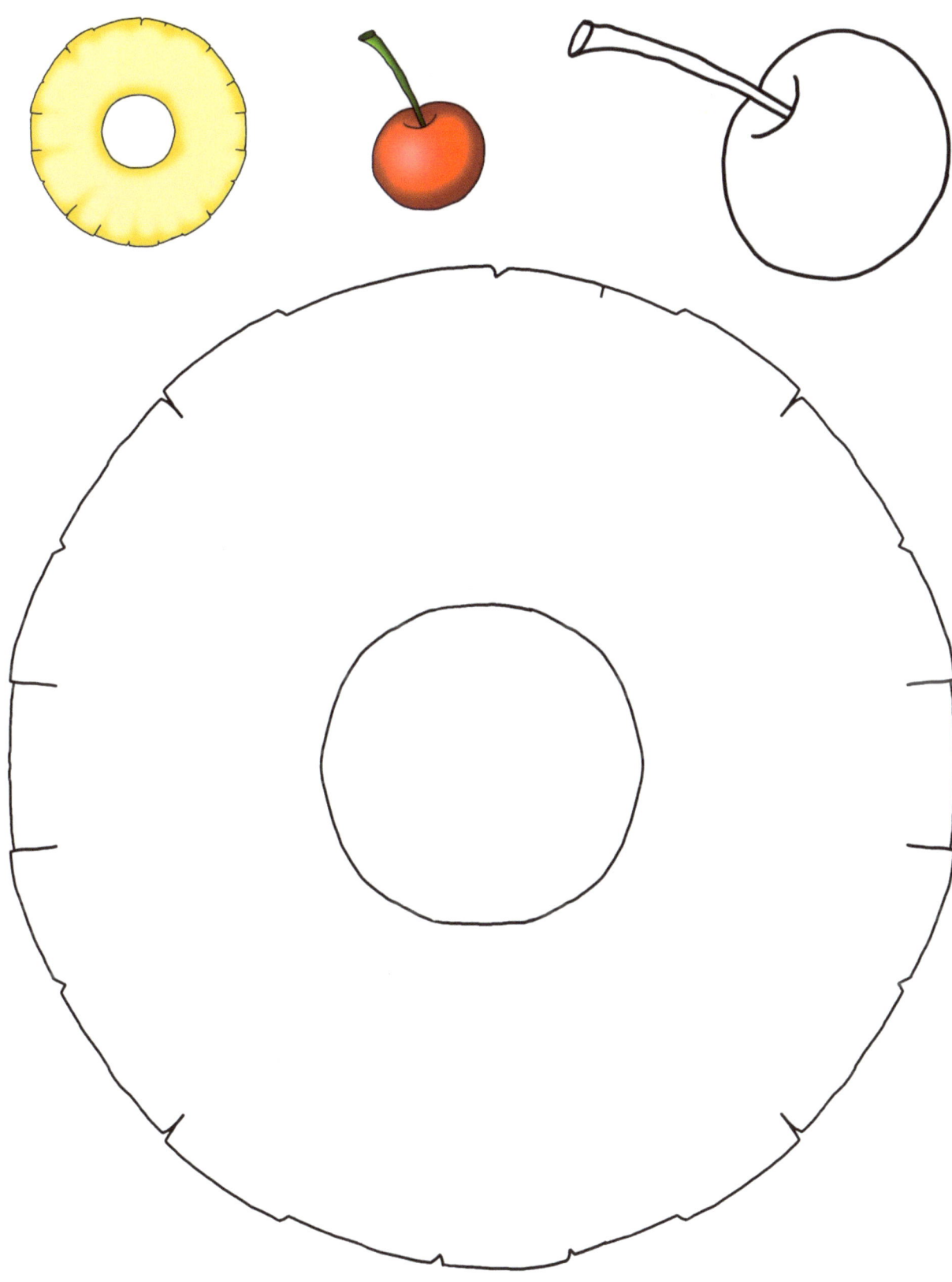

PINEAPPLE PASSION

PINEAPPLE PASSION

PiNeapple PassioN

PINEAPPLE PASSION

PINEAPPLE PASSION

PINEAPPLE PASSION   Copyright (C) Annie Lang

PINEAPPLE PASSION

PINEAPPLE PASSION

Pineapple

Copyright (C) Annie Lang

PINEAPPLE PASSION

Surf's Up

Surf's Up

(C) Annie Lang   anniethingspossible.com

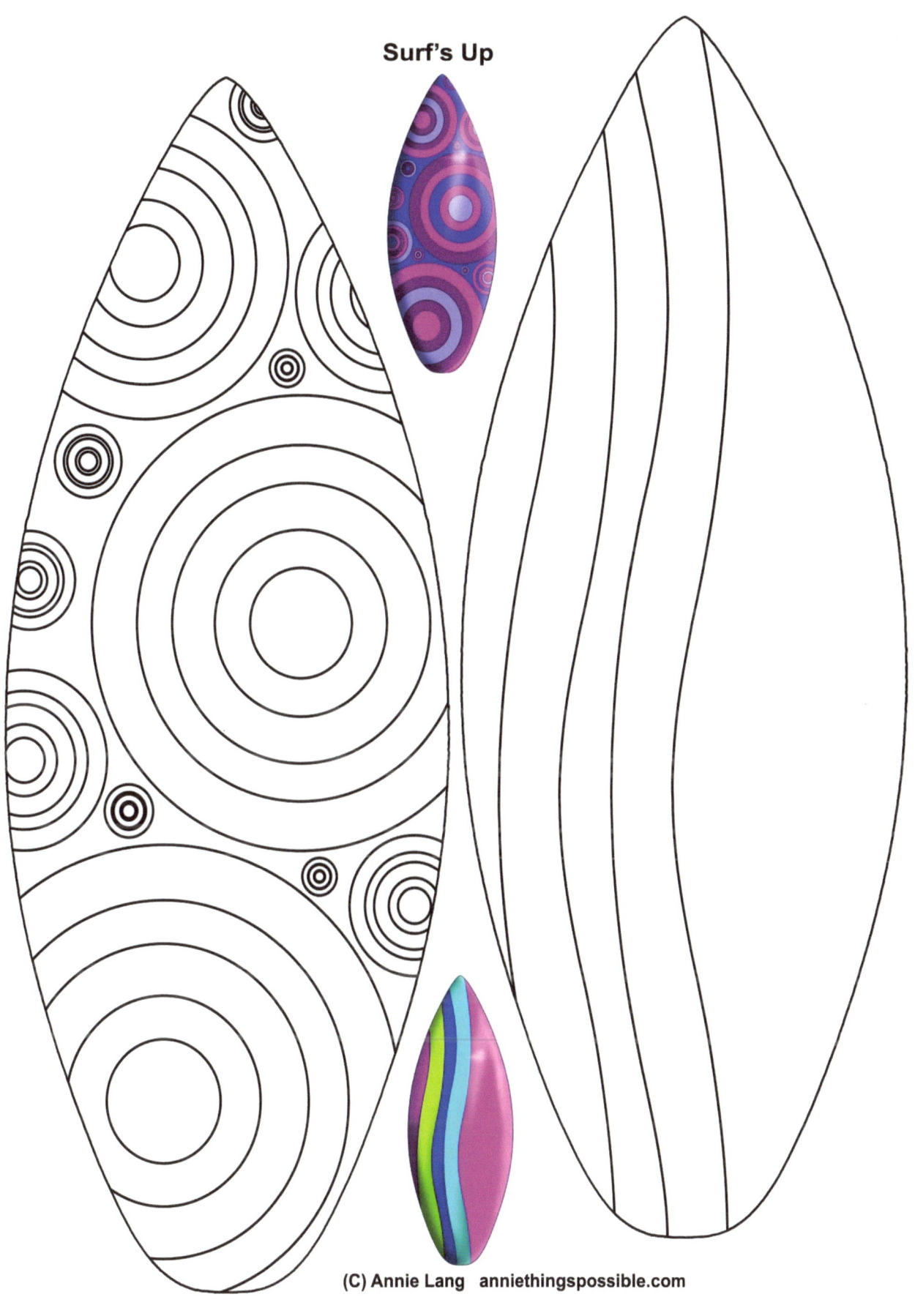

Surf's Up

(C) Annie Lang   anniethingspossible.com

Surf's Up

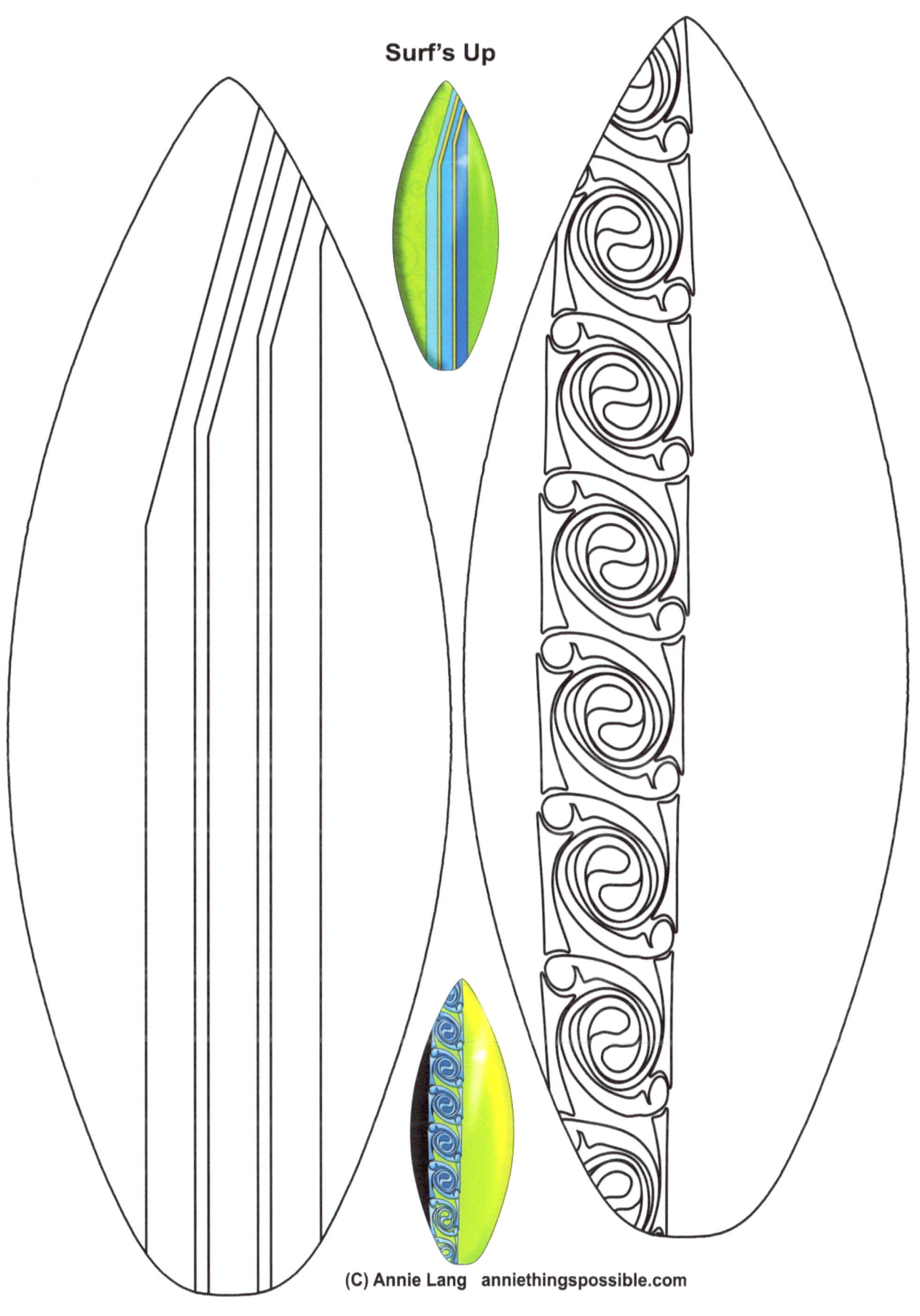

Surf's Up

(C) Annie Lang   anniethingspossible.com

Surf's Up

(C) Annie Lang   anniethingspossible.com

Surf's Up

(C) Annie Lang

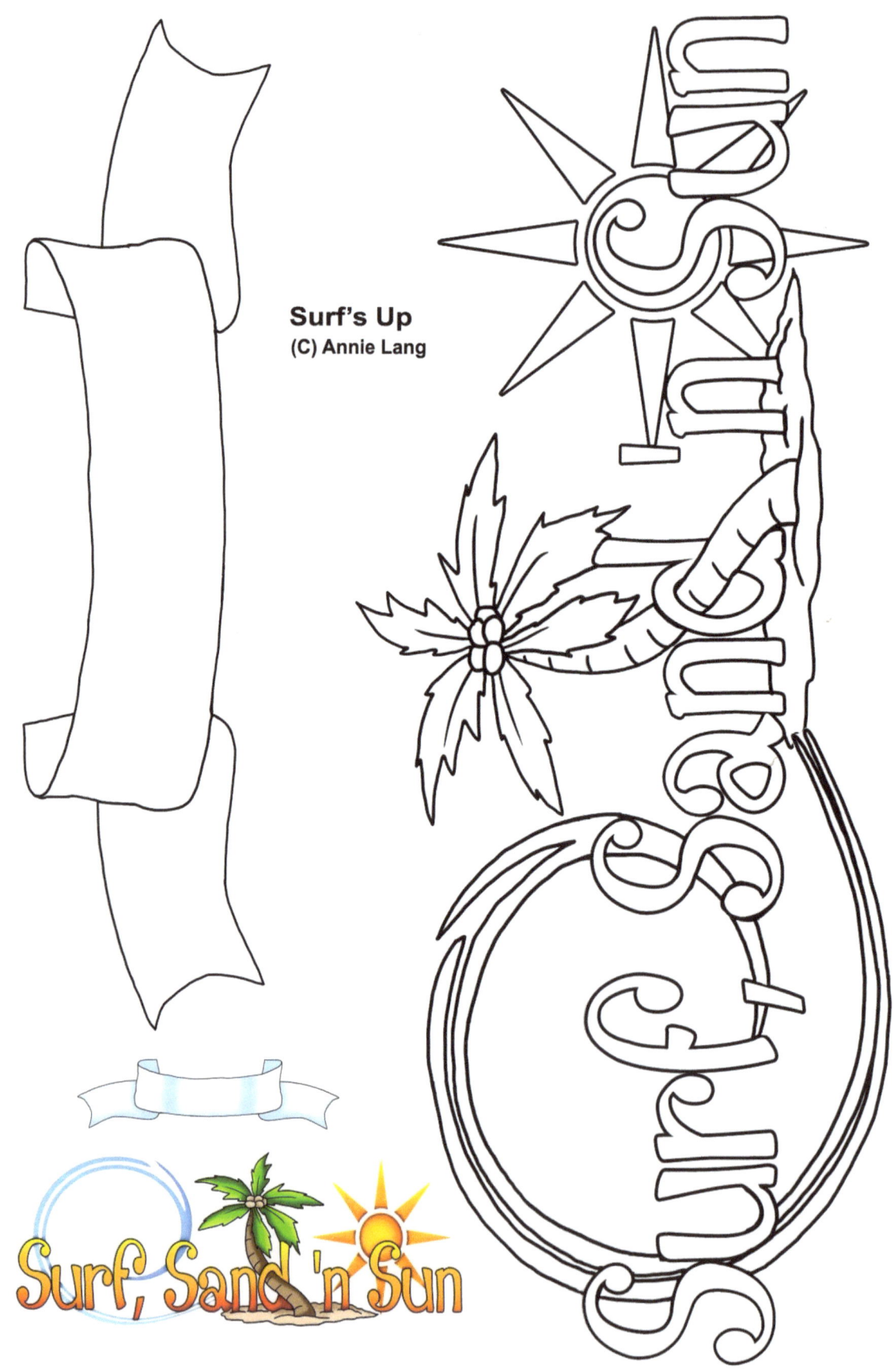

Surf's Up
(C) Annie Lang

Surf, Sand 'n Sun

Surf's Up

(C) Annie Lang

Surf's Up

notes and memos

Thank you for purchasing this publication!

Find dozens of other fun titles on my
Annie Lang's Books website!

I hope you enjoyed this book and
encourage you to leave a review and share your
thoughts for other customers at Amazon.com!

To learn more about the author, get free project
ideas, see video how-to's and more, please visit
Annie Lang's BLOG at
http://annielang-anniethingspossible.blogspot.com/